My Beauty Box

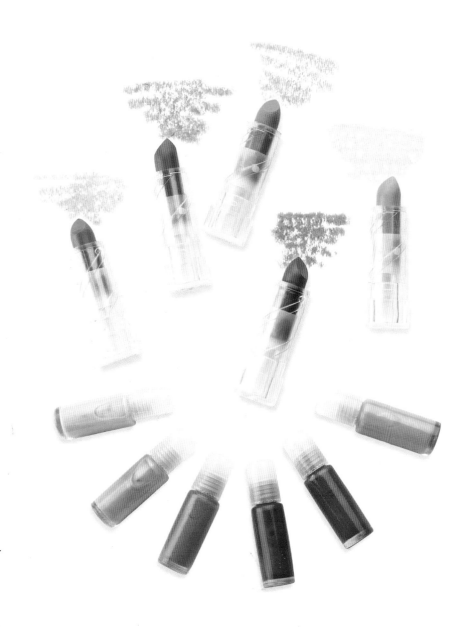

My Beauty Box

Christine Green

This is a Parragon Book

This edition published in 2003

Parragon
Queen Street House
4 Queen Street
Bath BA1 1HE, UK

Designed, produced and packaged by
Stonecastle Graphics Limited

Text by Christine Green
Edited by Gillian Haslam
Designed by Sue Pressley and Paul Turner
Illustrations by Paul B. Davies
Photography by Roddy Paine
Art direction by Sue Pressley and Paul Turner

ISBN 1-40540-402-7

Printed in China

Contents

introduction

Welcome to the world of make-up! This book is filled with lots of exciting ideas for using coloured eyeshadows and nail polishes, body glitter and lip glosses that can transform you from a schoolgirl one day, into a modern-day miss the next.

Trying out different shades and varieties of make-up is fun, swapping ideas with friends and making each other up can turn a sleep-over into a beauty salon and who knows, you just might find yourself being snapped up as the next cover girl of your favourite magazine.

The only problem when you first begin to wear make-up is in finding the colours that suit you best, and then learning how to apply the different types of make-up correctly, but once you learn you won't forget. And just think – once you have your own collection of eyeshadows and nail polishes you won't need to borrow your mum's, or your sister's. Who knows, they might even ask to borrow yours!

One thing is for sure. From the moment you open this book and as you go through each chapter, packed full of

ideas, tips and suggestions showing you how to take care of your nails, how to apply eyeshadow, ideas for new hair styles, plus tips from some of the top beauticians, you'll never want to put the book down. So enjoy yourself exploring the world of make-up.

How it all began

Did you realise that make-up has been around for centuries? In the fourth century Greek women used to colour their eyebrows using bizarre recipes, such as a mixture of crocodile dung and honey dissolved in onion water – it sounds revolting and no doubt smelt it too! Thank goodness times have changed.

Throughout history, fashion-conscious young women have developed their own styles. From the bold eye make-up of the 1920s, when it was chic for every woman to have a beauty spot and whose hair was always styled into a short neat bob with the tiniest of fringes, to the 1960s, when most women resembled pandas with their pale complexions and dark eye make-up – not to mention their boyish cut hairstyles. And now in the twenty first century, fashion dictates that anything goes – well, almost anything – providing it looks good.

Basic Make-up Kit

If you have never worn make-up before then you will need one very important accessory – a make-up kit made up from the following:

POWDER BRUSH – a large soft brush used when applying face powder.

BLUSHER BRUSH – smaller than a powder brush, used when applying blusher.

OLD TOOTHBRUSH – perfect for smoothing over rough skin on the lips.

LIP BRUSH – painting on lipstick is easier when you use a thin lip brush.

EYESHADOW APPLICATOR – most eyeshadows come with these but it is always handy to have others. Cotton buds can also be used.

COTTON WOOL – has 101 different uses.

CHAPTER 1 Fab Nails

Do you bite your nails, do you nibble at them when you're nervous or are they so long they keep snapping? It doesn't really matter whether your nails are long or short, the most important thing is that they look neat and tidy.

But did you know that each nail is made up of the protein keratin, that during the summer nails grow faster than during the winter? Furthermore, each nail is made up of six parts:

1 Matrix – this is the control centre which houses all the nerves and blood vessels that help nourish the nail. New cells are also created here.

2 Nail bed – the part attached to the finger. This is where the blood vessels which help feed the nail are stored.

3 Lunula– also known as the "half moon". Look closely and you will see this paler part at the very base of the nail.

4 Nail plate – the part that sits on the top of the nail bed. It is made up of many thin layers, kept together by oil and moisture that help to keep it strong.

5 Free edge – the part that hangs over at the end of the fingertip.

6 Cuticle – this very thin piece of skin is formed around the base of the nail and protects it from any bacteria getting underneath the nail and damaging the new cells being made.

The Secret of Nail Shapes

Nails can also say a lot about the type of person you are. Take a look at your fingernails and see which of the following descriptions they match up with:

BROAD NAILS – you always speak your mind, but sometimes it can land you in hot water. So try and think before you speak in future.

SHORT NAILS – the life and soul of any party, you're always bubbling with ideas and your friends love having you around.

LONG, ROUNDED NAILS – you make a loyal friend. Always there when needed, you take time to listen to people. No wonder you are so popular.

LONG, POINTED NAILS – you would never dream of leaving the house unless you looked 101%, but most of the time it is because you worry what other people are thinking of you. Don't waste your energy, they like you however you look.

THIN, NARROW NAILS – people's nasty comments can really hurt you, but that is only because you're sensitive and have a caring nature. Try not to take everything too much to heart – words can't hurt you.

Taking Care of Nails

Now you know how your nails are formed, the next thing to learn is how to look after them.

• Your diet doesn't only affect your hair and skin, it can also affect your nails too and following a bad diet can often result in the nails breaking and the skin around them splitting. One of the most important vitamins for the healthy formation of nails is calcium, found in milk and dairy products, so make sure you include plenty of these products in your diet.

• When washing the dishes or helping out in the garden, make sure your nails are protected and wear rubber gloves.

• Keep your fingernails fairly short for school – long nails can break so easily or get in the way when you are doing your work.

• After washing your hands it's good to apply some handcream. It helps to keep the skin feeling soft and it's good for the nails too.

✗ Never use your nails to open parcels or packets. Always use a pair of scissors.

✗ Bitten nails never look attractive and if you can't stop biting them there are lots of anti-bite lotions in the shops that can be painted over the nails. They taste horrid but at least it stops you from biting them.

✔ Why not carry an emery board around and every time you are tempted to bite your nails, file them instead?

✔ Better still, paint your nails with a pale-coloured nail polish and once you see how pretty they look you won't want to bite them.

Nail Equipment

To have stylish nails it helps to have the right equipment:

COTTON BUD – for pushing the skin around the nails back, also useful for removing smudges of nail polish.

COTTON WOOL BALLS – to use with the remover.

CUTICLE STICKS – to use with cuticle cream.

CUTICLE CREAM – applied to the base of the nail to make it easier when pushing the skin back.

NAIL POLISH REMOVER – important for removing the nail polish. Available as liquid or as wipes.

EMERY BOARD – for filing the nails.

BASE COAT – gives the nails a smooth surface before applying the polish.

A Perfect Manicure

One evening each week, give your nails a five-minute manicure to help keep them looking chic.

1 Using an emery board, file your nails from the edges into the centre rounding them until they are oval in shape.

2 Dip your fingers into a small bowl of warm soapy water for a few minutes. This helps to soften the skin around the nail base and so makes pushing the skin back easier.

3 Dry your fingers and nails thoroughly.

4 Massage some cuticle cream on to the fingertips and, using a cotton bud, gently push the skin back.

Applying Nail Polish

If you want to apply nail polish, simply follow the next steps.

When applying nail polish, rest your hands on a table to give you extra support – you will need a steady hand.

1 Apply a base coat and leave to dry.

2 Beginning with the little finger, sweep one stroke of polish from the base of the nail up the centre to the fingertip. Then take another stroke of polish and run it up either side.

3 When all the nails are painted, leave them to dry before applying the second coat.

If you have any smudges, wipe them away with a cotton bud dipped in nail polish remover.

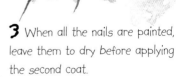

Deciding on Nail Colour

There are so many shades of nail polish that it can be a tough decision choosing which one to buy – from bronze to bright orange, from nail polishes that actually smell of chocolate or raspberry to others that shimmer and glitter once applied. Some nail colours even have holograms inside! The choice is yours. If you still can't decide, you could always create your own shades by painting one colour on top of another and sharing with a friend could double your colour choice! Different colours of nail polish definitely suit different types of nails, for example:

RED is a super colour for all nail lengths but not for bitten nails.

ORANGE, GOLD AND YELLOW look great on tanned or dark skins.

BLUE AND GREY – are cool, sophisticated colours.

SOFT PINKS are suitable for all nail lengths.

BEIGE AND IVORY colours are perfect for short nails.

Nail Fashion

Nail fashion is certainly the in thing at the moment. From peel-back tattoos and transfers that can easily be held in place on top of nail polish to fingernail jewellery, sparkling nail gems and nail art kits that make super birthday presents, you can have a really wild time experimenting with different looks.

False Nails

Do you wish you had really long nails that you could paint in different colours for special occasions? Well you can, only you have to buy them and take them off again. I'm talking about false nails, they're great to wear and can be decorated over with tattoos to look even more like the 'real thing'.

Some moulded plastic fingertips slide over your finger whilst others are basically the nail itself which is attached to your own nail and held in place with a peel-back sticky tape. The only thing you have to be careful with is when it comes to sizing up the nail shapes with your own but you can have a great time fooling everyone how quickly yours have grown, especially if you buy some tattoos to wear over the top.

The Family Gathering

Going to a family occasion and your parents don't want you wearing the latest blue nail polish just in case it gives Gran a shock? Why not apply a clear coat of polish and then sprinkle some coloured glitter lightly over the top.

1 Apply a base coat to each nail.

3 Before the polish has had a chance to dry, sprinkle coloured glitter over the top of each nail.

4 When dry, paint another clear coat of polish to hold the glitter in place.

2 Then paint a coat of the clear polish over the top.

This design is simple to achieve and looks really smart. Don't forget when putting the glitter over the nails to hold a sheet of paper underneath to save spare glitter for the next time.

Party Time

This is the type of nail effect that will have all your friends asking how you got the look. Don't tell them immediately, keep them guessing!

1 Choose a pale shade of polish in green or lemon.
2 When the first coat is dry, for a totally different look apply over the top one of the new polishes that actually has hologram stars inside.
3 Leave the nails to dry for about 20 minutes.

Nail Designer

If you want to be noticed, be artistic and design your own nail patterns. Here are some ideas you might like to try.

1 Paint each nail with one base coat.
2 Choose two of your favourite nail colours, one light, the other darker.
3 Apply a dark coat of polish and when dry apply a second coat over the top.

4 Leave the nails to dry for at least 20 minutes, then using the lighter shade of polish carefully dab little dots over the top.

Chess Board

Be bold, be beautiful and be recognised with this criss-cross design. However, it might need the help of a willing friend. Choose two different colours, one of which should be black, the other could be green, red or white.

1 Apply one coat of white polish on each nail. When dry, apply another coat.

2 This is where a steady hand is required. Before the second coat is completely dry, use a toothpick to score the criss-cross design onto the nail.

3 You will need a friend to help with this part. Apply black nail polish in every other square, so one will be white, the next one black, the next one white and so on.

The end result is amazing and if you felt really daring you could match up your eye and lip make-up the same way.

French Look

If you want to make heads turn try creating this very fashionable 1950s' look. It really does look lovely but it may take you a while to achieve perfection.

1 Apply a *base* coat over the nails.
2 Beginning just above the moon, very carefully draw a stripe of red nail polish up the centre of the nail.
3 Then apply another coat to each side.
4 When dry, apply a *second* coat.

Sparkle Party Nails

If you are going to a disco you will certainly stand out with this look but once again, you may well need the help from a friend to create it.

1 Apply a dark-coloured nail polish, such as deep blue or even black if you feel really brave.
2 When dry, apply a second coat.
3 Whilst it is still sticky use a pair of tweezers to place some tiny finger jewels on the nail. Arrange them in a zig-zag, or some other design. Allow to dry thoroughly.

Removing Polish

Chipped nail polish looks awful so make sure you remove your nail polish before it begins to chip. Dip a cotton wool ball into the nail remover and bring it from the base of the nail to the tip holding it to the count of five. This gives the remover ample time to soak in and bring the polish off smoothly.

To remove any traces of polish from the surrounding skin area dip a cotton bud into some remover. Remember: never apply new nail polish over old.

Top Tips For Top Nails

* Store nail polish in the fridge to stop it becoming too thick.
* Give your nails a weekly manicure. It keeps them looking nice and also encourages them to grow both longer and stronger.
* To strengthen weak nails before filing, give them a coat of clear nail polish.
* Prevent the top of your nail polish from sticking by rubbing some Vaseline around the top of the bottle.
* Pale nail polish makes short nails look longer.
* Darker colours make nails look shorter.

CHAPTER 2

Lovely Lips

Lips need lots of attention to prevent them from drying out, which is where lipstick, lip balm and lip gloss come in very useful.

Unlike other parts of the body that have oil-producing glands to help protect the skin, the lips don't, so they need special care. Lip balms, glosses and lipsticks not only add colour and shine to the lips but also give them moisture to prevent them drying out and becoming sore and cracked.

Taking care of Lips

The weather is number one enemy to the lips, causing them to crack, dry out and sometimes bleed, so what can you do?

DRY LIPS – during the winter months keep the lips well moisturised with lots of lip gloss. If you don't have any lip gloss, use Vaseline (many top models use this trick).

CLEAN LIPS – if your lips feel dry, give them a quick cleansing treatment to get rid of all the dead skin cells on the surface. Gently brush an old clean toothbrush over the surface in circular movements then apply some lip balm afterwards. You will find the lips feel nice and smooth.

CRACKED LIPS – because the skin covering the lips is so fine it can easily flake with small cracks appearing which can be very painful. So always protect them with lip balm or Vaseline during the day and before going to bed.

COLD SORES – not only can cold sores be painful but some people are prone to them every winter. The best advice is to protect them by wearing lots of lip balm.

SUNSHINE – lips don't like the sun as it dries them out, so just make sure you give them lots of protection with lip balm (choose one with UV protection).

Equipment

You might not need
much equipment for
the lips but it is just
as important:

LIP GLOSS – adds
a shine to the lips,
great to wear on top
of lipstick or alone.

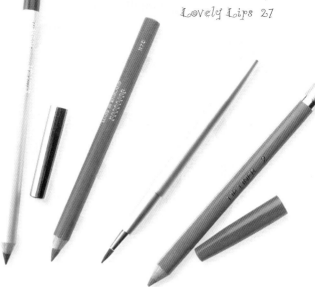

LIP PENCIL – used for
outlining the shape of the lips.

LIP BRUSHES –
used for applying
lipstick.

LIP BALM – gives added
protection to the lips.
Vaseline is just as good.

LIPSTICK –
adds colour and
helps moisturise the
lips to prevent them
drying out.

Lippy Time

The one problem in wearing lipstick is in getting it to stay on all day as it can be a pain having to keep reapplying it, but there is now lip sealer available which promises to keep those lips looking lovely and luscious all day long.

But if you don't like wearing lipstick, try wearing lip gloss or lip balm instead. You can take your pick of which colour or even flavour lip gloss you prefer from lemonade, mandarin, strawberry, even raspberry ripple, but the only problem is lip gloss doesn't remain on all day so it needs to be reapplied constantly. Or for protection against the elements, you might prefer to slap on some lip balm that again is available in lots of different flavours and good news for chocoholics – there is even a chocolate-flavoured lip balm.

Choosing the Colour

You've spent ages looking for a lipstick, trailed around endless shops, tried out nearly every colour you thought you liked and yet you still can't decide. If you find yourself facing this problem try this clever little tip which a top beautician uses: pull down your lower lip and look at the colour on the inside. If the skin is really pink then pinks, blues or other cool shades will suit your colouring. But if the skin is more of a salmon colour, then brown or gold shades will generally suit you best.

And if you still aren't convinced, most young skins suit browny pink shades, gold colours look cool on tanned skin and if you still feel confused, play safe and wear lots of shiny lip gloss.

Applying Lip Liner

The reason for using lip liner is to define the shape of the lips and it also helps to keep the lipstick in place. But first of all you must know how to apply it correctly:

1 Choose a colour more or less the same shade as your lipstick.

2 Apply lip balm to smooth out the lips.

3 Very carefully draw around the outline of the lips.

4 Now it's time to apply the lipstick.

Applying Lipstick

If you've never applied lipstick before don't worry. Just sit down with a mirror, take your time and follow these four steps:

1 A lip brush is the best way of making sure all the lips get fully covered, but don't worry if you haven't got one – use a cotton bud instead.

2 Dab the brush on to the lipstick and, keeping inside the outline you have already drawn, colour in the lips.

3 When complete press a tissue against the lips. This helps the lipstick remain on for longer. Then apply another coat.

4 Now it's time for a coat of lip gloss.

Different Looks

You'll be surprised at how creative you can be with lip colours. With a little imagination you can have your lips looking as wild and wacky as the rest of your make-up or as cool and chic as you like. Here are some looks to try out:

Hot Hot Lips

Feeling totally outrageous, do you want to make everyone stand back in surprise when you walk into the room? They will if you choose a blue or orange shade of lippy and to make them shine, slick on loads of lip gloss.

Glittery Lips

Why go to the expense of buying glittery lipstick when you can make your own for half the price? Cover the lips with Vaseline, then using the fingers, because it's easier and you won't waste so much, dab some loose face glitter over them.

And if you're going to a party and have got glitter over your hair, your shoulders and your arms, then what about the lips? Apply a beige lipstick and dab some loose face glitter over them. You'll sparkle.

Natural Look

The easiest way to make your lips look natural is to choose a shade of pink and cover with Vaseline or lip gloss.

Brighten up your Lips

Slightly bored with your lipstick but you can't afford to buy another? Don't worry – try this idea. Put a shimmery pink eyeshadow on your bottom lip and also on the cupid's bow (in the middle of the top lip) – it does the trick and saves you buying another lippy.

Party Time

Outline the lips with an orange lip pencil or use your lip brush covered with some lipstick if you prefer. Paint the rest of the lips with orange lipstick and dab some gold coloured lip gloss on to the centre of your bottom lip. It will look sensational.

Top Tips For Top Lips

* Never throw old lipsticks away. When you have quite a number, put the remaining pieces of lipstick into a glass bowl over a pan of hot water and heat very gently. You must do this with the help of an adult. The pieces will melt and you can then stir them into a half-empty pot of lip balm and there you have a new lip gloss.

* Store your lip pencil in the fridge for about 20 minutes before sharpening. This makes a much sharper point.

* If you don't have a lip brush use a cotton bud to apply your lipstick.

* Dark colours make the lips appear thinner, pale colours make them look fuller.

* Never lick the lips as this only dries them out.

* Lipstick and lip gloss will last forever but if you notice they begin look past their best, throw them out.

CHAPTER 3 Bright Eyes

Did you know that eye make-up is the most popular type of cosmetic and with literally hundreds of different colours and shades from which to choose, imagine how much fun you can have deciding which one to buy.

Taking Care of Your Eyes

Have you ever wondered how some people's eyes are always so bright and sparkling? It's probably because they look after them by making sure they get enough sleep and take plenty of healthy, outdoor exercise. Sometimes the eyes can feel tired and sore for no reason. If this happens to you, cut two thin slices of cucumber and place one over each eye. Lie down on your bed and listen to some music for ten minutes or so – you'll be surprised how refreshed your eyes will feel afterwards

Puffy Eyes

A late night can often result in bags appearing under the eyes the following morning and although you would love to go back to bed unfortunately it's a school day. Don't worry, pop a clean damp flannel into the freezer for about ten minutes, place it over the eyes and lie back on your bed for five minutes, and no one will ever know you had a late night.

Equipment

MASCARA – used for darkening the eyelashes. Available in a range of different colours, brown or black are generally most popular for daytime.

CLEANSER – available in cream or lotion forms and used for removing make-up. Choose one which is suitable for removing eye make-up.

COTTON BUDS – ideal for blending different coloured eyeshadows.

COTTON WOOL PADS – important for using with the cleanser when removing eye make-up.

Wearing Glasses

If you wear glasses don't think you can't wear eye make-up, because you can – you just need to think a little more carefully about the colours you choose.

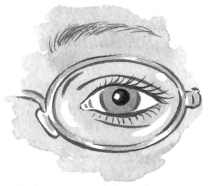

Generally if the glasses make your eyes appear larger, choose softer coloured eyeshadows that won't draw attention to them, such as beige or mauve. If, however, the glasses make your eyes appear smaller then you can be daring and choose bright bold colours which will draw attention to the eyes. And don't forget loads of mascara!

One more tip: if wearing mascara, make sure it has dried thoroughly before putting your glasses back on, otherwise it might smudge over the lenses.

Making-up

When you first begin to wear make-up it can be confusing to know where it should be applied. So take a look in a mirror and learn to identify different parts of your face.

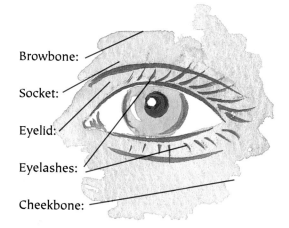

Browbone:

Socket:

Eyelid:

Eyelashes:

Cheekbone:

Applying Eyeshadow

Applying eyeshadow isn't always as easy as it seems, especially if you have never done it before, but it can be great fun practising. Most experts advise that when you first begin using eye make-up that you should experiment using neutral shades, as coloured eyeshadows are slightly more difficult to apply. So make sure you are sitting with a mirror in front of you and have fun.

1 Sweep the applicator over the eyeshadow and stroke it over the entire eyelid.

2 Blend it in with a cotton bud until it looks even.

Mixing Colours

If you can't decide which colour eyeshadow to buy, follow these useful tips:

• If you have bluey grey eyes, yellow, orange or a coppery colour look good.
• If you have green eyes, a plum coloured eyeshadow will make your eyes stand out.
• To emphasise brown eyes, use pink, salmon or a taupe coloured eyeshadow.

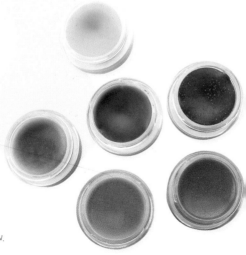

Two or More Colours

The fun can begin when you decide you want a different look and want to use two shades.

1 Sweep the applicator over the darker eyeshadow and apply it as you did before but this time you can make it look slightly darker.

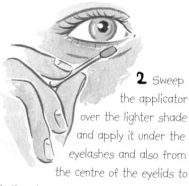

2 Sweep the applicator over the lighter shade and apply it under the eyelashes and also from the centre of the eyelids to both outer corners.

3 And don't forget the mascara.

Always make sure you blend the colours in well using either a brush or, if you find it easier, use your finger (first, just make sure it is clean).

Applying Mascara

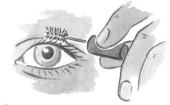

1 Dip the wand into the tube and, looking directly into the mirror, apply one stroke of mascara from the roots to the tips of the top eyelashes.

2 Then brush the mascara wand from the roots to the tips of the lower lashes.

3 If you want to apply a second coat, wait until the first has dried.

If you find you smudge mascara when painting the lower lashes, hold a tissue underneath.

False Eyelashes

False eyelashes can look flattering and they're great fun to wear but can be difficult to apply so you may need the help of a friend.

1 Always apply them *before* any eyeshadow.

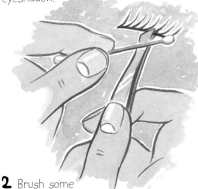

2 Brush some mascara on to the lashes. Hold the false eyelashes with tweezers and use a cotton bud to dab a tiny bit of eyelash glue (this should come in the pack with the lashes) at both ends of the band.

3 Leave it to dry for a *second*. Pick the eyelashes up with a pair of tweezers and place them carefully on the eyelid over your own eyelashes.

4 Press the lash band down on to your eyelid.

5 Once the glue has dried use an old clean toothbrush to brush over the eyelashes.

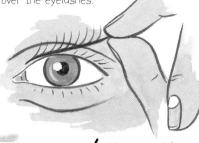

6 To remove false eyelashes gently peel them straight back, beginning at the outer edge.

Dotty Eyes

This look is so easy to create and you can have a wild time choosing which colours to use.

1 Cover both eyelids with two coats of white eyeshadow.
2 Use a grey eyeshadow and sweep this along the eye socket towards the outer corner of the eye. Blend it in with a brush.
3 Take a black eye pencil and firmly, but gently, draw dots over the eyelids.
4 To complete the look, add coats of mascara.

Flattering Eyelashes

If you are going to a party and only want a hint of colour on the end of your lashes, use a different colour, such as indigo or blue, and wipe it only on the tips of your lashes.

Party Eyes

Treat yourself to some body glitter or sequins to finish off this stunning look.

1 Blend a dark, shimmery eyeshadow with Vaseline and apply it with your finger along the socket line.
2 Make the eyes shimmer by dabbing some glitter gel into the centre of each eyelid.
3 The final touch is to brush some body glitter over the cheeks.

Glitter Mad

Treat yourself to some eye sequins for this great look.

1 Cover the eyelids with a stunning gold eyeshadow.
2 Apply two coats of black or brown mascara.

3 And for an extra sparkle, stick a couple of sequins at the side of the eyes, holding them in place with Vaseline.

Daytime Look

If you don't want to wear too much make up, go for this daytime look.

1 Sleek a smoky grey eyeshadow across the whole eyelid.
2 Take it up at the corners to make the eyes appear bigger.
3 Then finally apply a coat of mascara.

Feeling Funky

If you want to be outrageous, this eye make-up is for you.

1 Apply a blue eyeshadow to the inner corners of your eyelids.
2 Blend in a red eyeshadow along the rest of the eyelids and up into the sockets.
3 The finishing touch -- lots of mascara.

Removing Eye Make-up

Removing make-up before going to bed is as important as learning how to apply it correctly. If you go to bed with make-up on it doesn't do your skin any good and can lead to an outbreak of spots and dull skin. If you don't want this to happen use a gentle cleanser last thing at night to get rid of every bit of make-up. You'll be glad that you did.

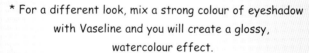

Top Tips For Top Eyes

* For a different look, mix a strong colour of eyeshadow with Vaseline and you will create a glossy, watercolour effect.

* When eyeshadow is past its best don't throw it away; dampen it and use it as an eyeliner, applying with a fine brush.

* To make sure you have used up every last bit of mascara, stand the barrel in warm water for several minutes before use.

* If you want powder eyeshadow to look darker, dip the brush into some water before applying the shadow.

CHAPTER 4 Healthy Hair

It doesn't matter if your hair is short, long, straight or curly, there are lots of different things you can do with it.

Are you bored with your current hairstyle and want a change? Do you wish your hair was longer or a different colour, perhaps you wish it was shorter and you didn't have to bother too much with it? Some people spend a fortune having their hair coloured, adding extensions to it, sitting under dryers for hours, getting it permed when you really don't need to. All you really need to do is to learn to be inventive.

Caring for Your Hair

To have healthy hair, it is important to look after it and so that means:

- Make sure you have regular trims.
- Sand and chlorine both damage the hair so whenever you go swimming or to the beach, make sure that you rinse the hair thoroughly.
- Following a healthy, well-balanced diet with plenty of fresh fruit and vegetables will make sure you have healthy shining hair.

Equipment

These are the essential items of equipment required:

BRUSHES – those with long, widely spaced bristles that will not get tangled within the hair are the best types. The smoother and blunter the bristles, the kinder they will be to the hair. One way to check is to press the brush into your palm – if it hurts, choose a brush with blunter bristles.

COMBS – good quality plastic ones with teeth spaced wide apart so they won't tear the hair.

HAIR DRYER – Choose one with a range of heat and speed settings.

There are lots of other things on the market that can be used when styling the hair. It helps to know how to use them properly:

SERUM – used for adding shine to dry hair, smoothing down styles and separating curls. Never use too much otherwise it will make the hair look greasy.

MOUSSE – ideal for adding volume to fine hair; also ideal for calming down frizzy hair. Don't use mousse on dry hair otherwise it will make it go crispy.

GEL – used for sculpting the hair into a certain design, ideal for short styles. Never apply too much – you only need a ball about the size of a 10p coin.

HAIRSPRAY – used for keeping styles in place. For an even coverage try spraying onto your brush first. When spraying, don't use the hairspray too close to the hair otherwise it will make the hair sticky.

But before you can make sure you take care of your hair you should know what type of hair you have. There are three main types but some people have combination hair:

NORMAL HAIR – shiny and easy to manage. **HELP** – use a mild shampoo and a light conditioner.

GREASY HAIR – looks flat and oily. **HELP** – use a shampoo for greasy hair. Apply light conditioner to the ends.

DRY HAIR – looks dull, and is difficult to brush; may snap easily. **HELP** – use a shampoo for dry hair with added moisturiser. Condition after every wash and leave hair to dry naturally.

COMBINATION – may be greasy at the roots and dry at the ends. **HELP** – use a mild shampoo. Apply conditioner only to the ends.

AFRO CARIBBEAN – can sometimes be dry and fragile and so needs extra care. **HELP** – apply a gentle shampoo and a rich conditioner.

Hair Problems

DANDRUFF – this is a build-up of dead skin cells lying on the scalp that often falls on to clothes. The best treatment is to use an anti-dandruff shampoo.

FRIZZY HAIR – in order to stop hair becoming frizzy, use a gel when your hair is wet. Blow-drying the hair slowly is also important.

SPLIT ENDS – the only treatment is to have them cut off.

Shampooing

If your mum has always washed
your hair, you might feel that the
time has come for you to do it
yourself. One of the most important
things is to use a shampoo that
matches your hair and to wash it as
often as is necessary in order to keep
it looking clean and shiny. Using too
much shampoo won't make the hair
any cleaner; it can actually make it
look dull so as a general rule, short
hair only requires a very small
amount of shampoo, longer hair
needs slightly more.

1 Brush your hair until it is smooth
and free from tangles. Bend over a
basin and wet it thoroughly.

2 Pour some
shampoo into the
palm of your hand
and after diluting it
with a small amount of
water rub the palms together
to work it into a rich lather.

3 Apply the
shampoo to the scalp and using
the fingers in small, circular
movements, massage the shampoo
into the hair for several minutes.

4 If you
have a shower
attachment,
lean over the
basin and use this to rinse
the hair, otherwise use a large jug.
5 Cover the head with a towel to
absorb most of the excess water.

Conditioning

Not everyone finds it necessary to use a conditioner; some shampoos already have them added. But if you do have to use one, the time to apply it is after the hair has been washed.

1 Apply it to the ends of your hair and then comb through gently.
2 Leave it for a minute or two before rinsing clear with warm (not hot) water.
3 Pat hair dry with a towel.

Hot Oil Treatment

This is ideal for someone who has dry or Afro hair that needs extra conditioning. A hot oil treatment is good to do once a month or when you get together with your friends and have a sleep-over.

1 Measure two tablespoons of olive oil into a cup. Pop the cup in a bowl of hot water until the oil has gently warmed.
2 Massage the oil into your hair.
3 Place a piece of clingfilm around your hair and scrunch it up to seal the ends.
4 Wrap a towel around your head and watch TV or listen to some music for half an hour.
5 Shampoo well and rinse.

Drying

Leaving the hair to dry naturally whenever possible is always better than blasting it with a hair dryer. However there are occasions when you will want it dried quickly and for those occasions it is important to do it correctly.

1 Make sure the hair isn't totally wet. A quick rub over with the towel will get rid of excess moisture.

2 Put some mousse or styling product through the hair to safeguard it from the heat of the dryer.

3 The sections of hair you aren't drying should be clipped away on top of the head.

4 Only dry small parts of the hair at any one time. Beginning at the back, place the brush around a section of hair. As you pull the brush through, move the hair dryer at the same time down the length of hair. It should be held approximately 10cm away from the hair and on a high setting, then when the hair is nearly dry reduce the heat to medium.

5 Once that section is dry move it to one side, pick up another section of hair and dry it in the same way.

6 Continue doing this on small sections of your hair until you have worked your way around to the sides. Then let down the hair that has been clipped up and do the same with the top layer, working from the back around to the sides.

7 Don't hold the dryer too long over one section of hair otherwise it could singe it. Keep moving it, curling the hair around the brush as you do so.

8 If you have a fringe, it will be the last section to dry.

Blow-drying can be tricky to begin with but a good way to master the technique is to do it on your best mate's hair and then she can do yours!

Finger Drying

This is so easy to do and is great for short hair because it gives the hair lots of height.

After combing your hair into the style you want, run your fingers through the hair quickly and, at the same time dry it, lifting and curling the hair into the direction you want it to hold. If you have very fine or flyaway hair that just refuses to keep any style apply some mousse to the hair before you begin drying.

Scrunch Drying

If you want to give your hair a wavy look, try this method.

1 Apply plenty of mousse.
2 Tip the head forward and point the hair dryer at the roots
3 With your head still forward grab handfuls of hair in your fist and dry it bit by bit.
4 Don't brush the hair or you will ruin the curls. Just spray them with hairspray to keep their shape.

Hair Accessories

Whatever style or length of hair you have, there are sure to be some accessories on the market that you can use and which will only cost pocket money to buy.

SCRUNCHIES are really popular and brilliant for wearing to school, especially as there is a wide variety of colours and styles available. Some have cute attachments to them such as Indian feathers or small characters.

HAIRPINS are ideal for holding buns and chignons in place.

HAIRCOILS shaped as stars are attached to a metal coil that twists into the hair. Hairbeads look super in any length of hair and work by gripping the hair to keep the style in place.

BENDIES are flexible lengths of wire covered in fabric which have to be twisted to hold in place and look super in ponytails.

And don't forget, hairsprings, mini crocodile grips, clasps and hairbands always make perfect hair accessories and even stick-on jewels can all make a plain hairstyle look extra special.

When plaiting the hair use wool, or interweave ribbon, even long scraps cut from an old dress would look good. Instead of buying a bandanna, make your own using a broad piece of material: tie a big bright ribbon around your hair and pull wisps of hair through; borrow some of your younger sister's beads and use them to attach to your hair. And if you really want to be trendy the newest craze for ponytails and perfect for those discos with flashing lights is to tie the hair into a high ponytail and spray loads of hair glitter into it.

If you are short of money and could do with some new hair slides, dig out some old ones that are looking slightly the worse for wear and paint them with your nail polishes so they match up.

Colouring Hair

It isn't a good idea to dye your hair when you're young. It is much better to keep to your natural colour and leave all the dyeing and colouring until you are older. But this doesn't mean that you can't add a touch of colour to your hair. Hair mascara and hair lipsticks can add dramatic colour for a party and, even better, they wash out, just in case you don't like the look. Add some glitter to your hair and for a totally dramatic look spray on hair colour which is available in most shops and means you can have practically any colour you like.

Hair Styles

If you are bored with your current hairstyle and are looking for new hairstyles to try out, then here is a selection you'll love.

Long Hair

FUNKY

This style is more suited to hair of one length.

1 Make a zig-zag parting then separate the hair into two high ponytails.
2 Secure the ponytails with small hair bobbles. Wrap pieces of hair around the bobble leaving the ends spiking out.
3 For extra colour add some hair coils.

PLAITING

1 Brush through the hair and slip on a crocodile hair band until it fits neatly.
2 At the nape of the neck divide the hair into three sections. Begin plaiting halfway down and tie a bright band around.
3 And to jazz it up, try adding some hair gems.

WILD AND WACKY

This hairstyle will certainly turn the heads of all your friends.

1 Use a fine comb and part your hair into as many sections as you want.

2 Put each section into a ponytail using different coloured bands.

3 Plait each section.

4 Using face or hair paints and a very thin brush, paint in between the partings on the scalp.

5 If you prefer, buy some hair jewels and stick these on along the parting.

6 Then cover your eyes and give it a quick hairspray.

SOPHISTICATED LOOK

This design is definitely one to try when you are going out with the family or to a special party.

1 Brush the hair back into a high ponytail then twist it back on itself.

2 Pin it secure but leave the ends spiky.

3 Give it a quick squirt with some hairspray and then arrange the spiky ends.

Medium Length Hair

FUN FUN FUN

1 Brush your hair and take it up into a high bun.
2 Secure it with a small hair bobble, leaving the ends of the hair spiky.
3 Slip some pins in to hold it firm but leave bits sticking out.
4 Jazz it up by adding some funky hair accessories.

PRETTY TRESSES

This is an easy style to do and it doesn't matter what length your hair is.

1 Brush your hair and put some small crocodile clips in around the front.
2 Then spray some glitter over. Pretty, dead simple and very effective.

THE SPIKY LOOK

1 Make a parting down the middle.
2 Take each side back and secure them into a bun leaving the ends spiky. Then using some crocodile clips, insert them into the bun to add a little colour.

Short Hair

SLEEK LOOK

Don't imagine that if you have short hair that you can't spice it up – remember short hair looks neat and doesn't take long to wash! Temporary hair extensions can be added on and there are lots of different hair accessories!

1 Apply some gel evenly over the hair and sleek it back off your face.
2 Make a curl in the front or put some hair jewels into it.

MINI TWISTS

This style can be used on long, medium or short hair.

1 Separate the hair into lots of different sections. Then twist each section round and around until you can do it no longer.
2 To hold each twist in place slip two hair grips in, one going one way and the other crossing over. Leave spiky bits sticking out.
3 Don't forget the hairspray.

Braided Hair

This looks really cool on any length of hair but it definitely needs the help of a friend. It doesn't matter what colours or how many colours of thread you use. You might need to do some practising before you get it right but it will be worth it.

1 Take two lengths of embroidery thread approximately two and a half times longer than your hair. Imagine they are red and blue. Tie the ends together in a knot.

2 Comb a small section of hair close to the front of the head and carefully tie the knotted end of the thread around the hair.

3 This is the tricky part. Place the blue thread down alongside the hair and take hold of the red thread.

4 Begin winding the red thread around the hair.

5 When you have covered about 5cm pick up the blue thread, leave the red one, and begin winding this one around the hair until another 5cm have been covered.

6 Just take your time and keep on changing the threads all the way down the hair.

7 When you get to the end of the hair secure the ends by tying them in a small neat knot.

Keeping Hair out of Your Eyes

Ever wondered how some of the top pop stars manage to keep their hair out of their eyes when performing? Some of them wear cute slides at the side and others use a poodle bunch. Simply gather the front part of your hair into a ponytail and fasten it at the top with the band. Ideal for wearing at school.

Hairbands

There are loads of different size hairbands, stretchy ones, diamanté and crocodile hairbands, wide bands that look super on long hair and even those very thin hairbands. Better still, you can wear two together.

Top Tips for Top Hair

* Never tie hair back too tightly or secure it with an elastic band as it will split the hair.

* Never comb tangled hair from the roots. Instead, gently ease it down from the bottom and work your way up to the roots.

* Keep hair in good condition – have it trimmed every two months.

* Check out your local hairdresser to see if they have model nights when they are looking for young customers to try new styles out on. They won't cost you so much money because they are training but you had better check with a parent first.

* Never allow other people to use your brushes or combs and make sure you wash them regularly in warm soapy water, then leave them to dry naturally.

CHAPTER 5

And More...!

The basic make-up items have been covered in earlier chapters, but there are still other beauty products which you may want to use at some time in the future and so it is useful to know about them and how to apply them correctly.

Blusher

Adds colour to the face. Available in powder or cream. When applying blusher, begin at the cheekbones, sweeping the blusher over and up towards your temples. Blend the colour well towards the hairline so you avoid harsh edges. Don't put too much blusher on.

Tinted Moisturiser

Gives the skin a healthy glow. After washing your face apply the moisturiser, making sure it is blended in well so you don't get any streaky lines.

Shimmery Body Lotion

Glittery body lotion adds a sheen to bare shoulders. After a shower or bath, smooth it over the areas where the sun will catch it.

Face and Body Glitter

There are lots of different types of body glitter that look really cool on your shoulders, neck, arms and even your face. Some body glitters are available as roll on, others have to be put on with the fingers but wherever you put it make sure that you wash it off afterwards.

Face charms

There are lots of face charms available, such as dolphins, stars and various other shapes. They're easy to apply with Vaseline over any part of the body and they look great.

Tattoos

The favourite place for wearing temporary tattoos is around the ankle or upper part of the arm, but they can look trendy almost anywhere. There are lots of fun tattoos on the market which are simply rubbed over the skin with some water.

Bindis

These are very fashionable. They are often seen amongst Asian women worn on the centre of the forehead and they are so simple to apply. Just peel off the backing paper and stick on to the forehead for a night out.

Jewels

These tiny jewels look so pretty and can be carefully glued on to different parts of the body, but make sure that you always use the correct glue.

Freckles

Some people hate freckles but some models actually paint them on when they are required to do a job that calls for a fresh-faced look. Simply use a mid-brown eyebrow pencil and dot freckles over the nose and cheeks. Soften the edges of the freckles with a clean cotton bud before applying some loose powder to set the whole look.

Top Tips For Top Looks

* It isn't only the outside you should think about looking good. Remember to brush your teeth in the morning before going to school and again in the evening before going to bed.

* Always make sure you get a good night's sleep.

* If you have no blusher, dot a touch of pink lipstick on your cheeks and blend it in well.

* Many people have sensitive skin and for that reason buy hypoallergenic make-up. You can also buy hypoallergenic nail polish too.

* You don't always have to spend a fortune on buying make-up. Many shops' own label goods are very good value for money.

* Get together with a girlfriend and make each other up. It's surprising to find out how other people see you and who knows, you might even prefer that new you!

* Keep perfume strips from magazines in your sock drawer for a great fresh smell.

* If you want some advice about choosing the right type of make-up don't be afraid to ask one of the shop assistants. As long as you are polite they'll be delighted to help.

* To clean make-up brushes, wash them in warm water with some shampoo added. Then place them on a clean towel and leave to dry off thoroughly.

* To freshen up your skin and give it an overall glow, splash it with cold water. This is great for the circulation.

Make Your Own Make-up Box

In order to keep all your make-up together, store it in a bag or better still, why not cover an old shoebox with some colourful paper? In that way you'll have plenty of room and won't lose anything.

1 Cover an old shoebox with a sheet of pretty wrapping paper. Wallpaper would look just as good.

2 Make sure it reaches up all four sides before gluing it in place.

3 Take another piece of paper and cut it to fit inside the box, up the sides and neatly over the edges. Glue in place.

And there you have it, a super make-up box that will keep all your equipment together.